This Book Belongs To

Thank you for being our valued customer. We would be grateful if you shared this happy experience on Amazon. This Helps us to continue providing great products and helps potential buyers to make confident decisions

COLOR TEST PAGE

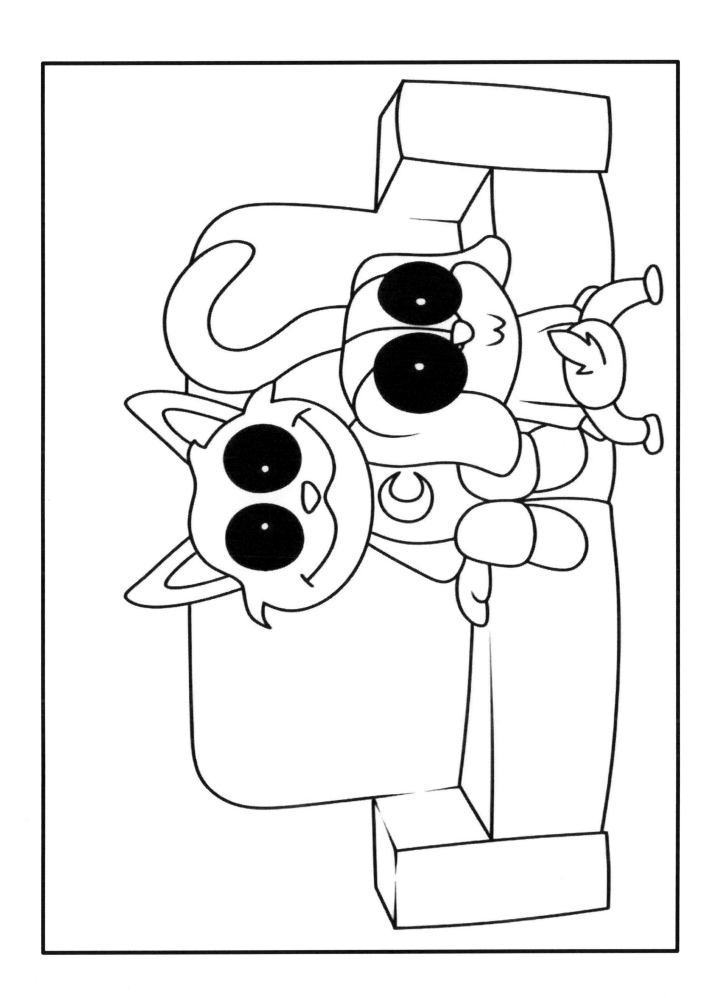

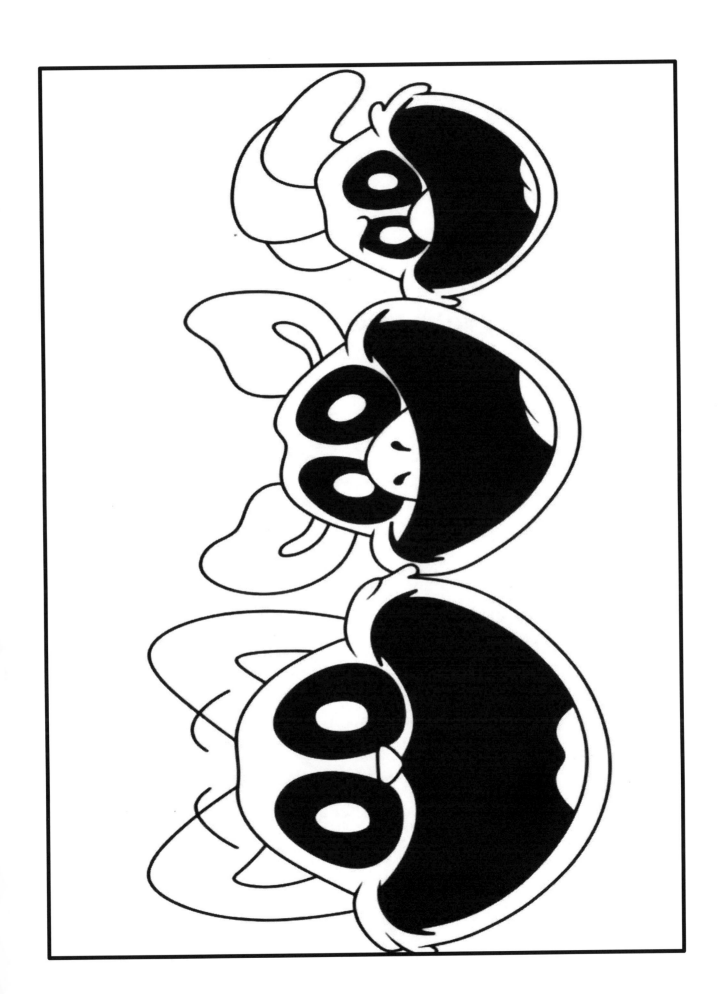

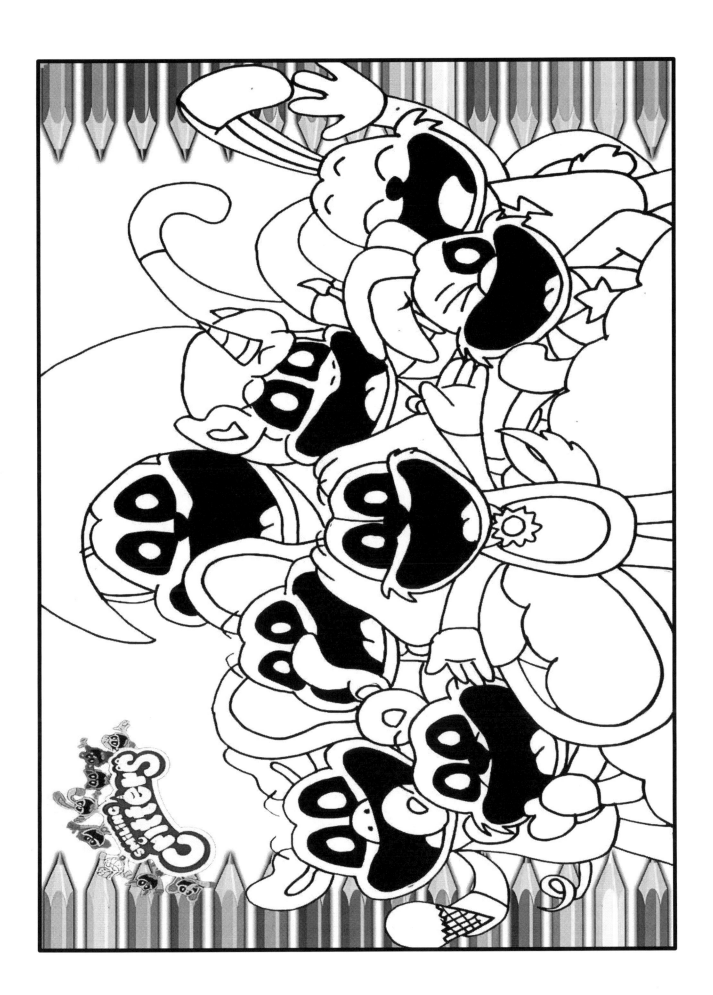

Made in the USA
Columbia, SC
14 January 2025